CHRISTMAS CATS COLORING BOOK

By
Go and Color

ISBN: 9781081141998

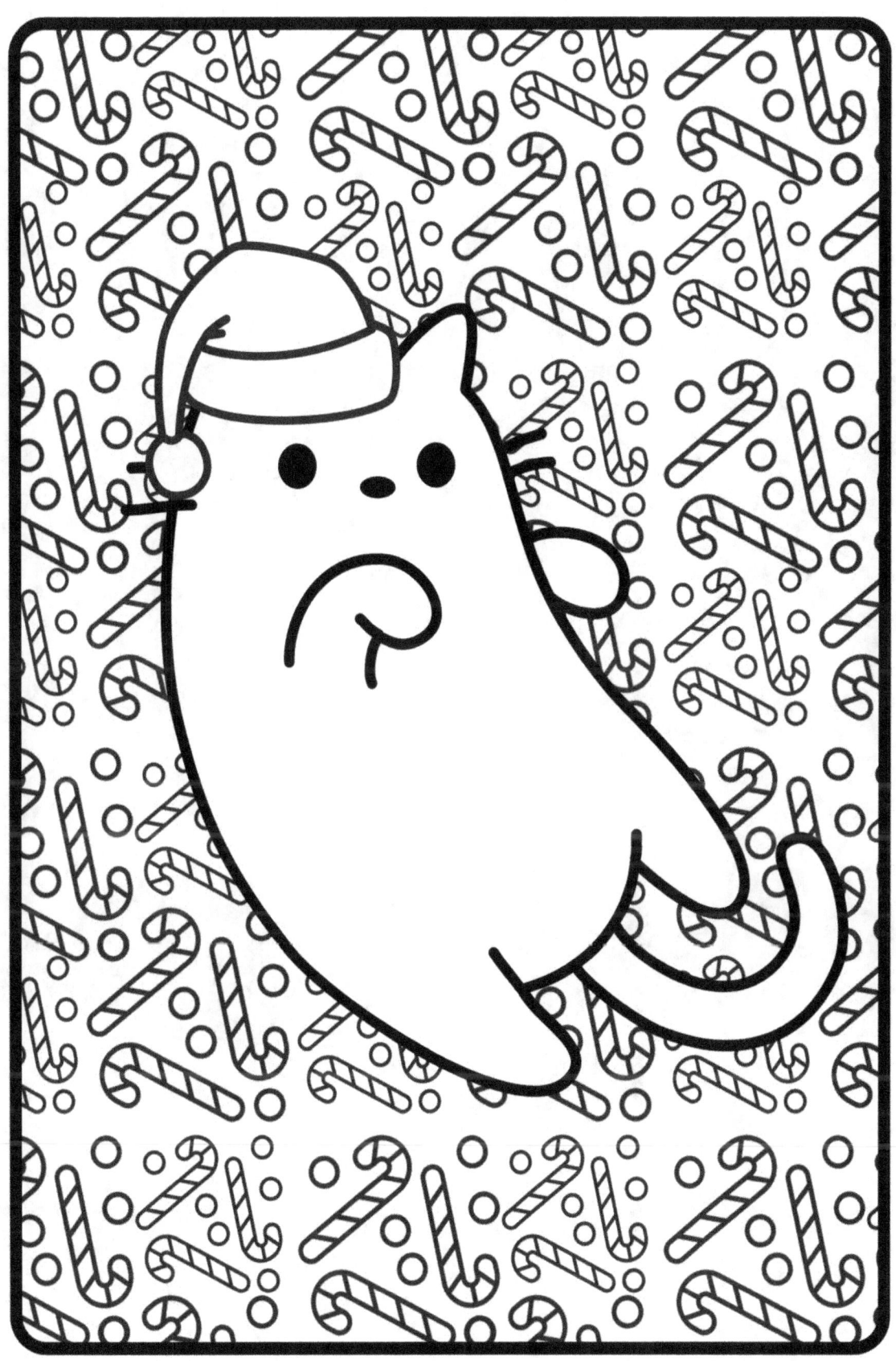

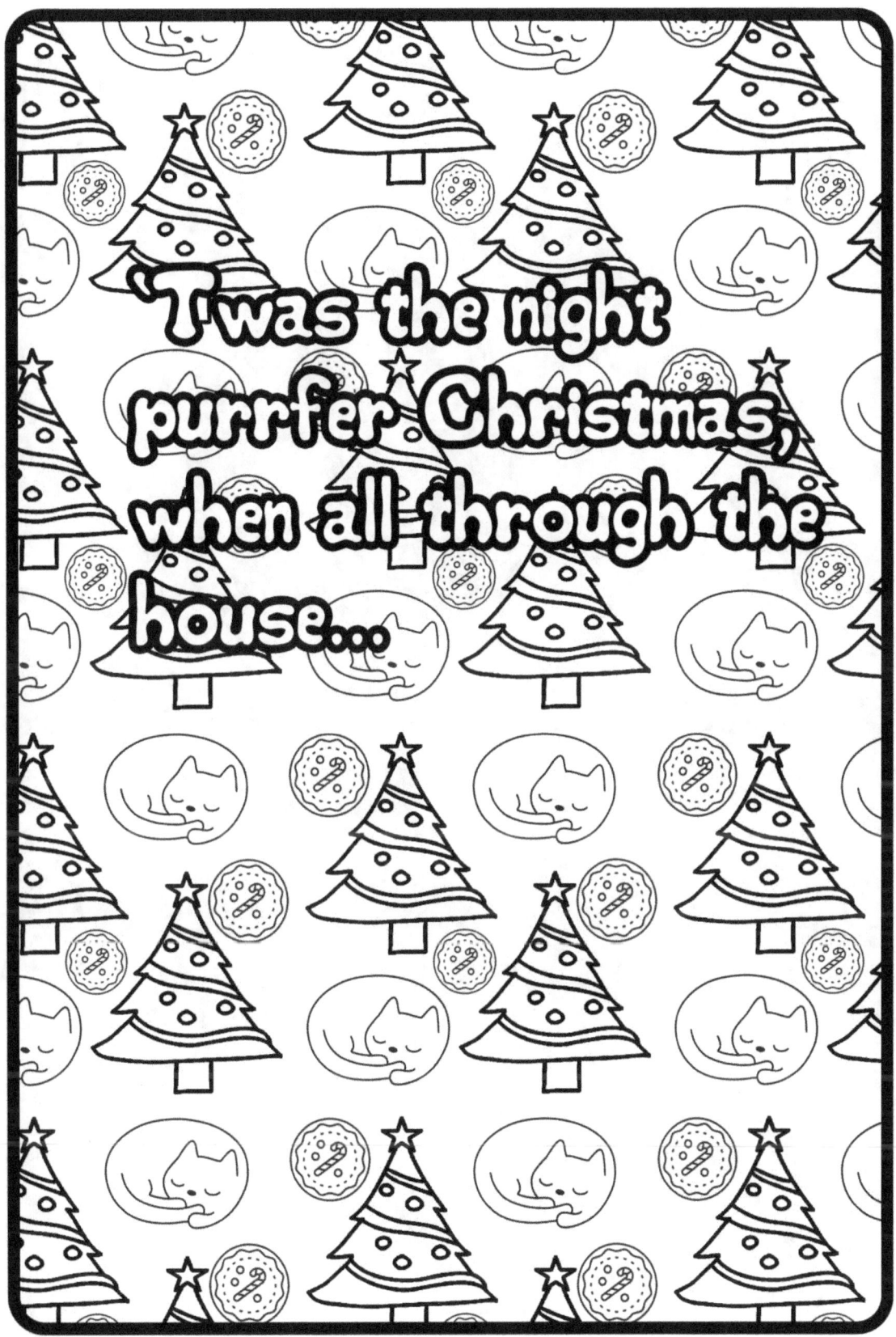

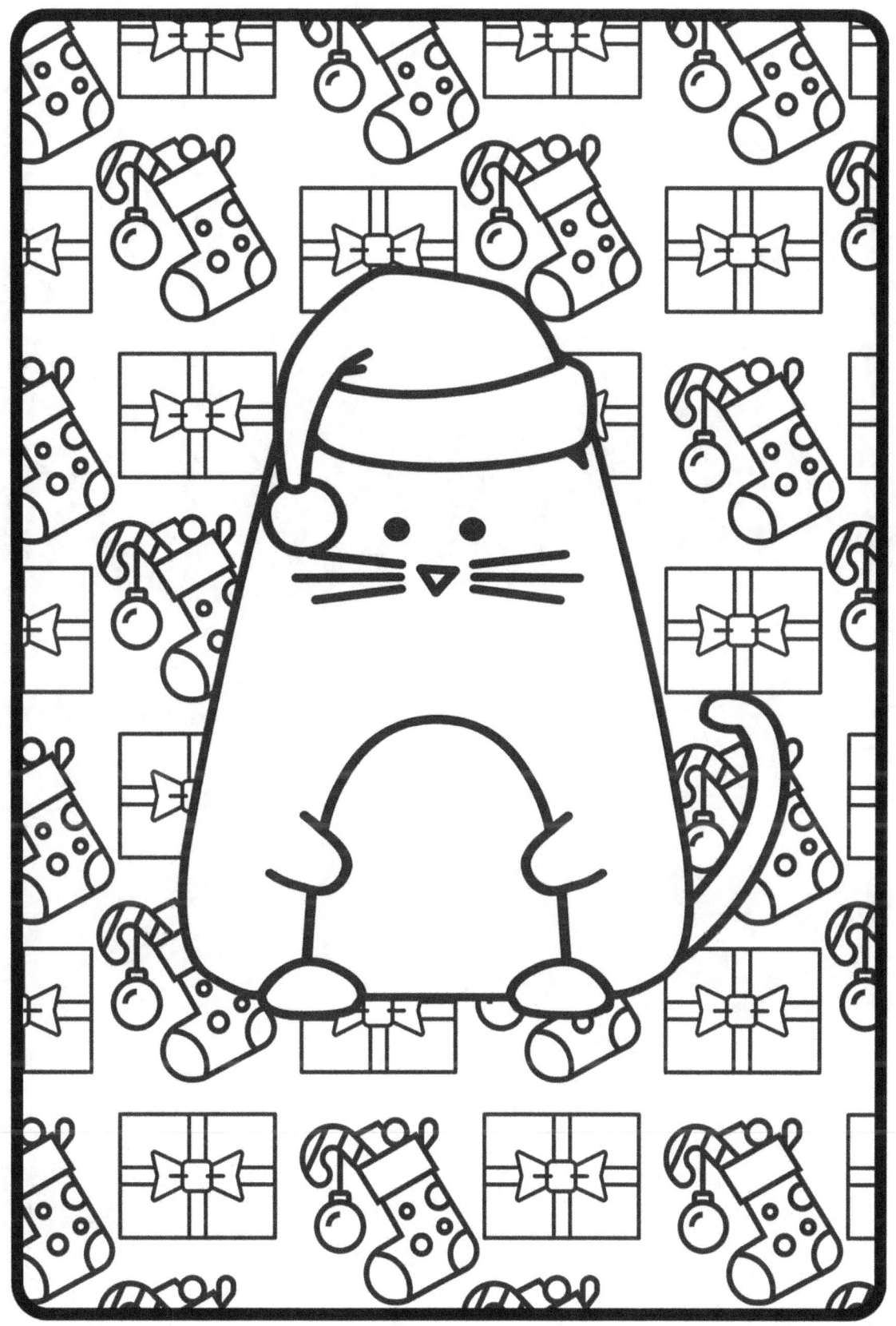

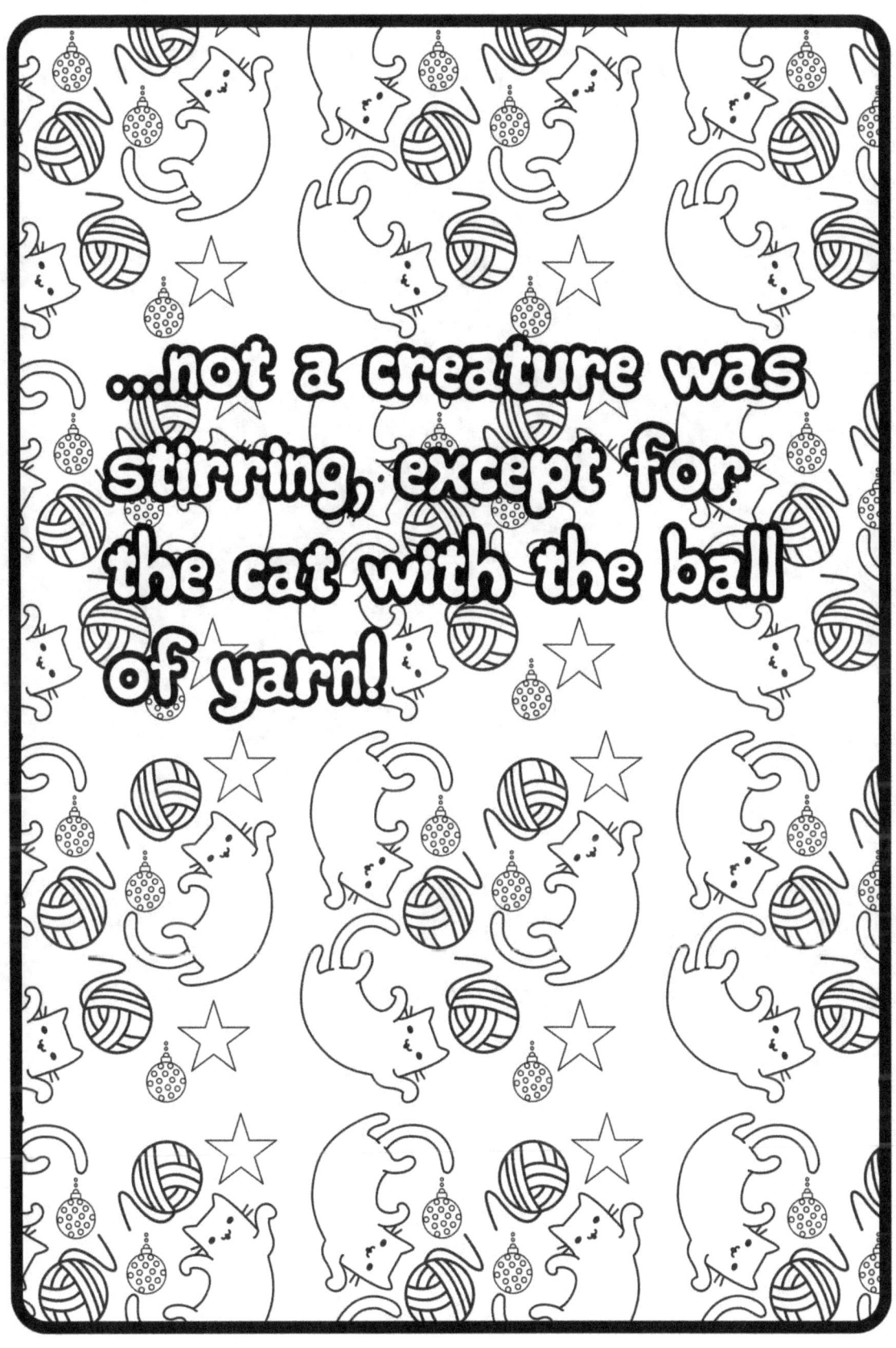

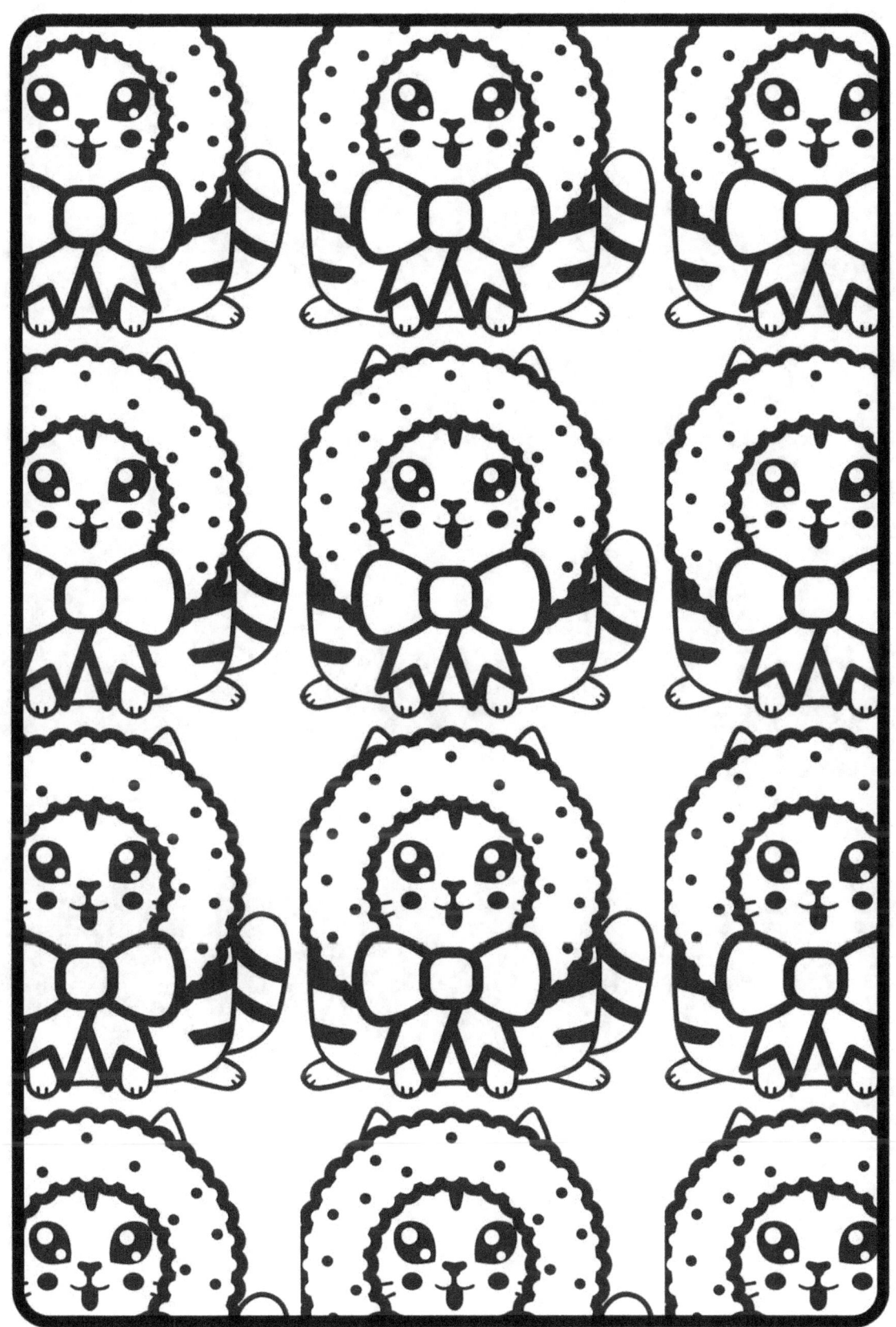

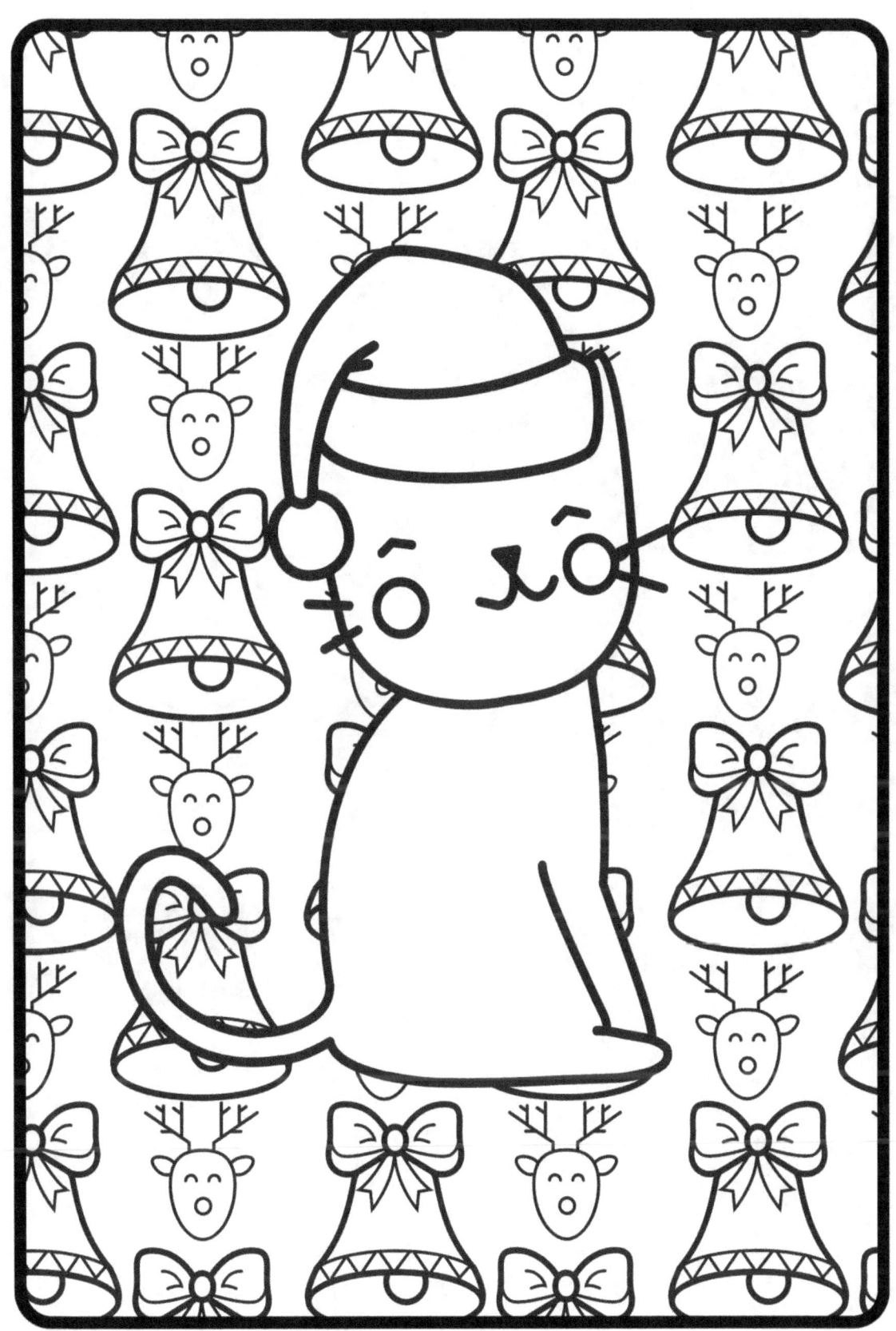

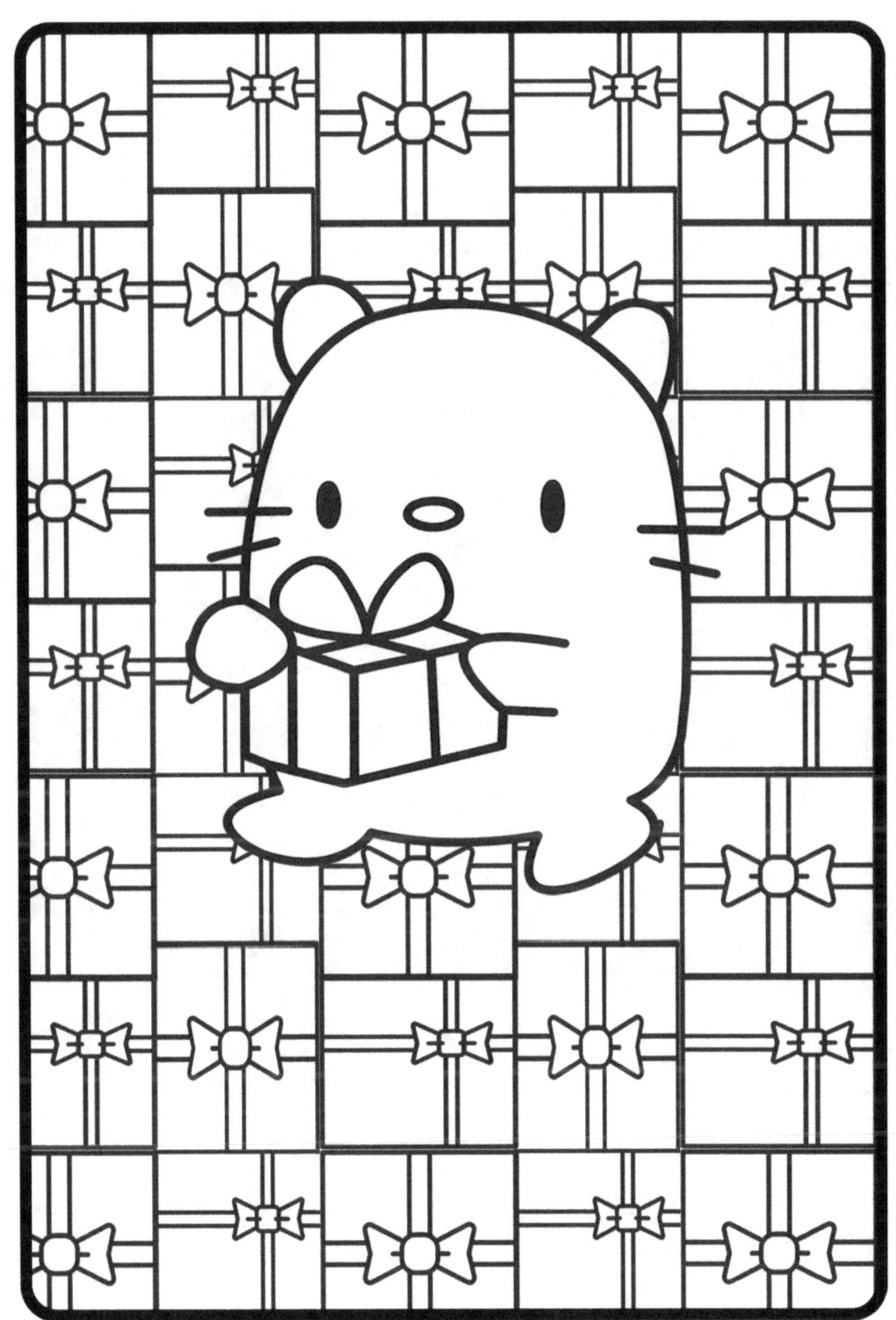

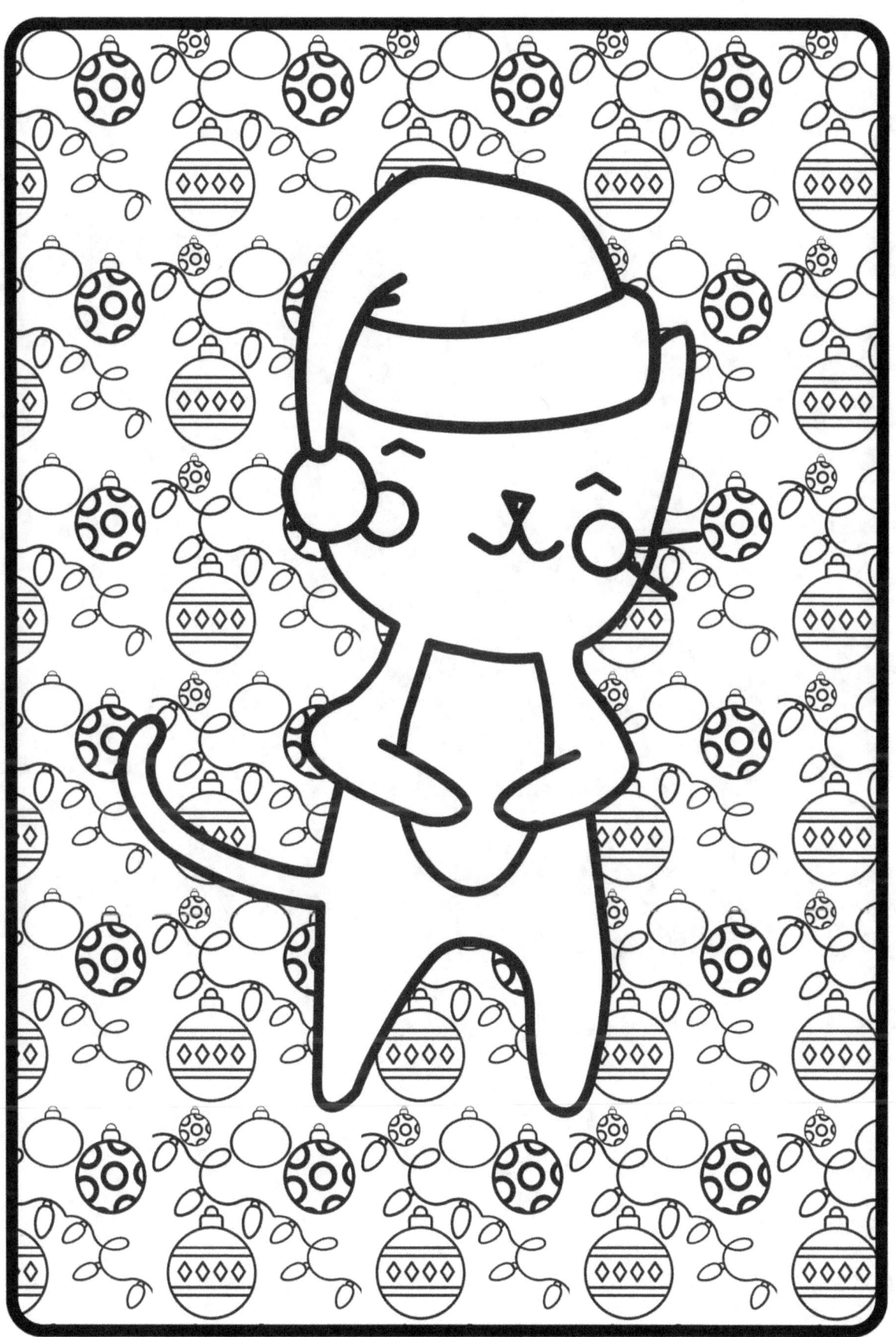

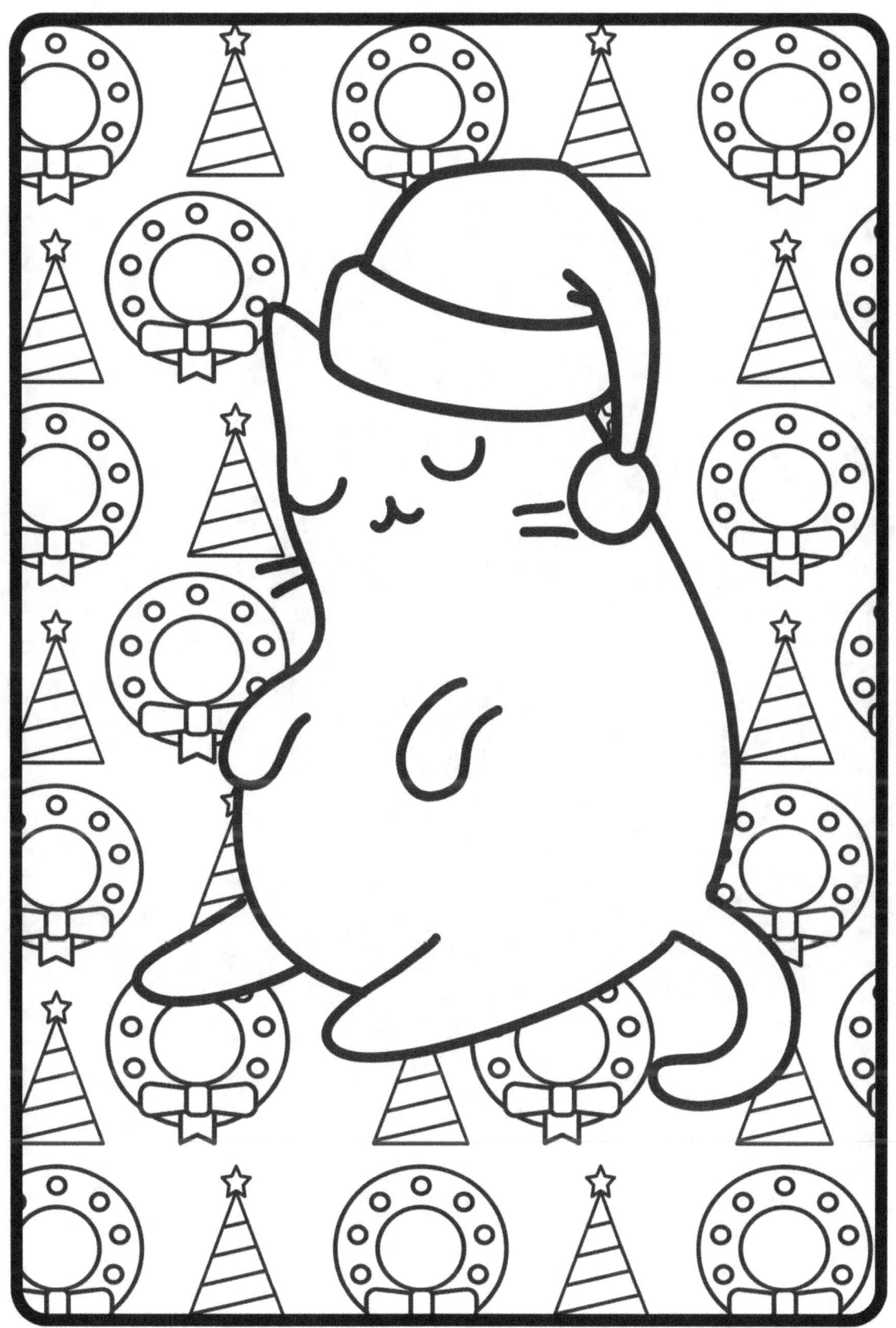

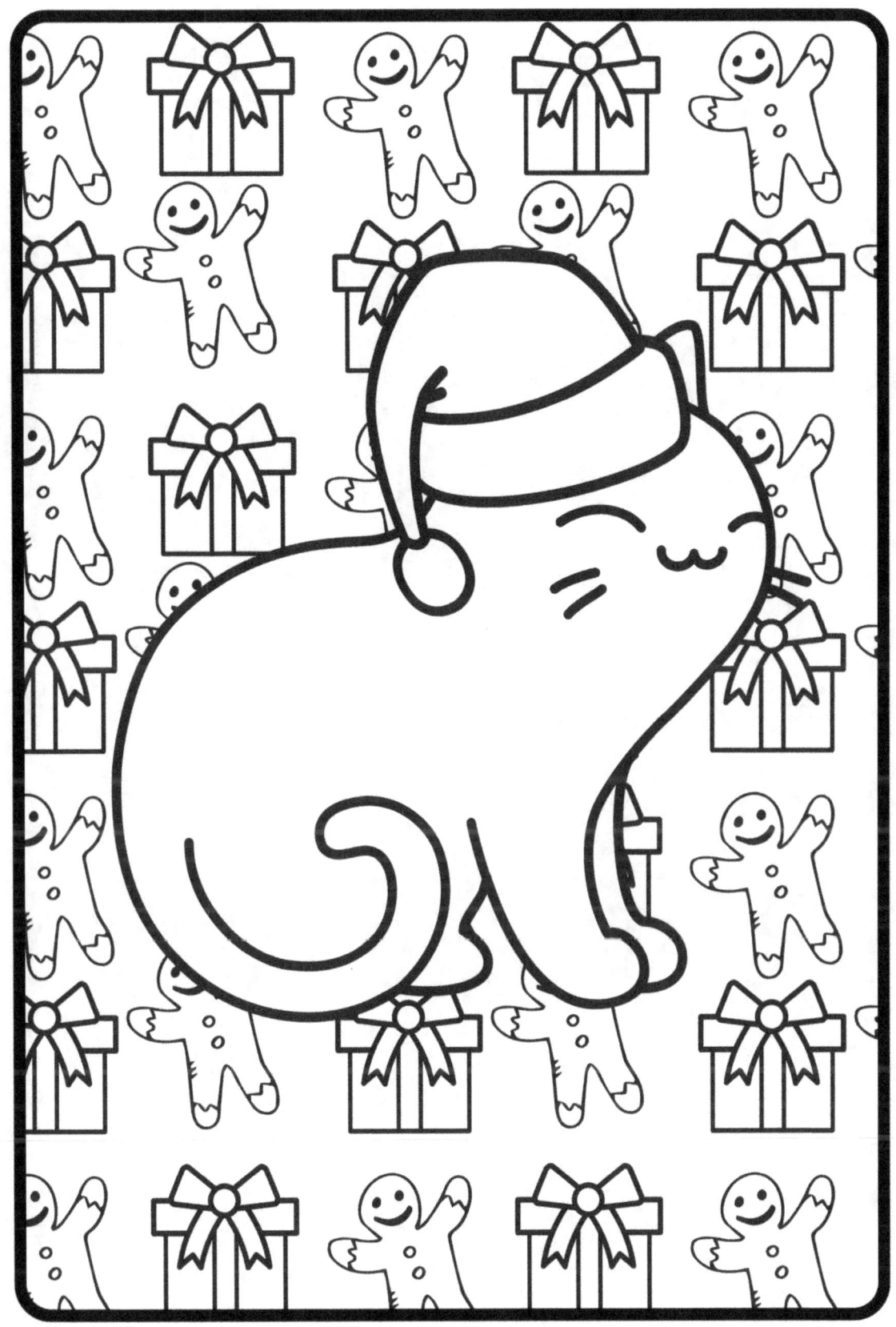

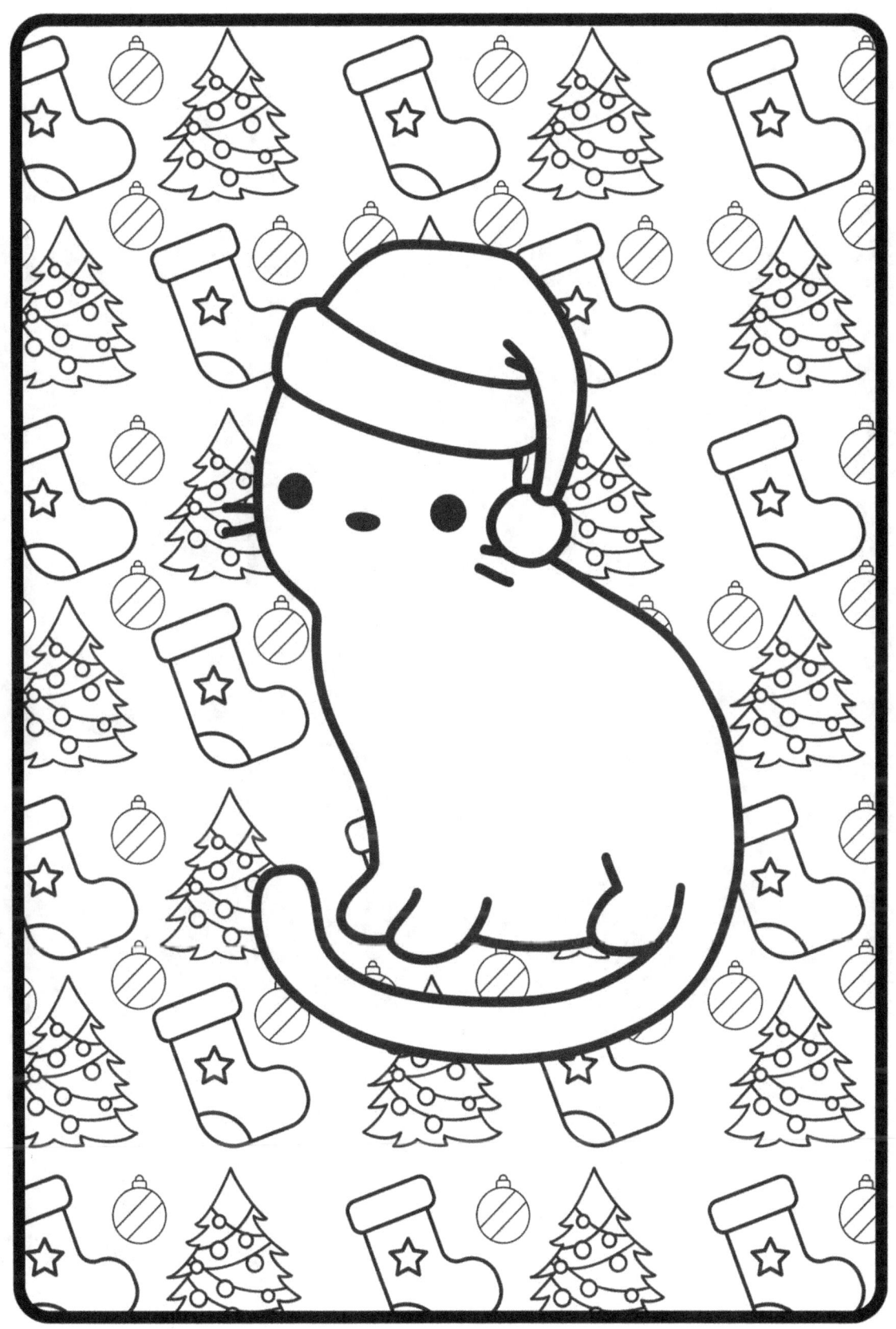

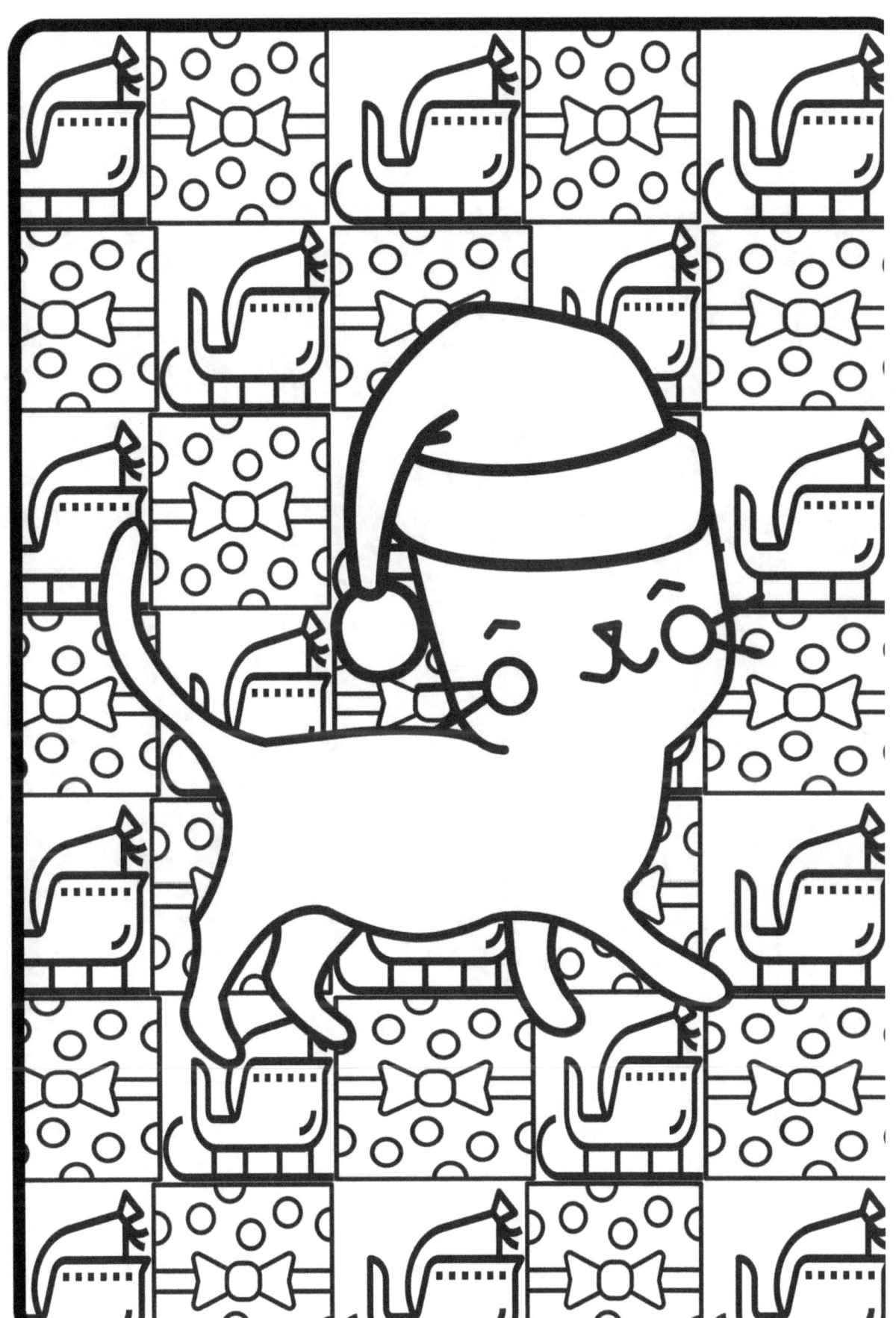

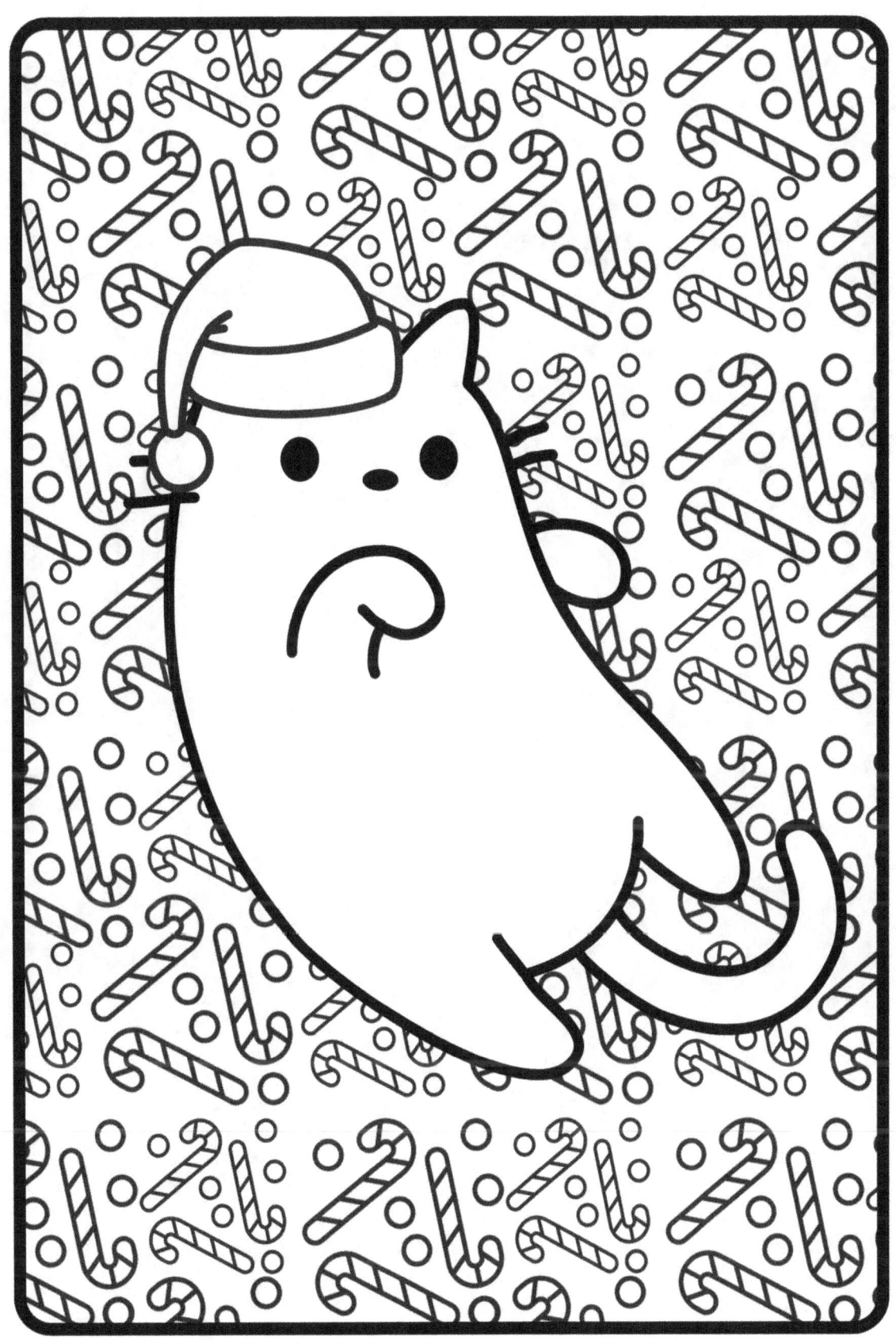

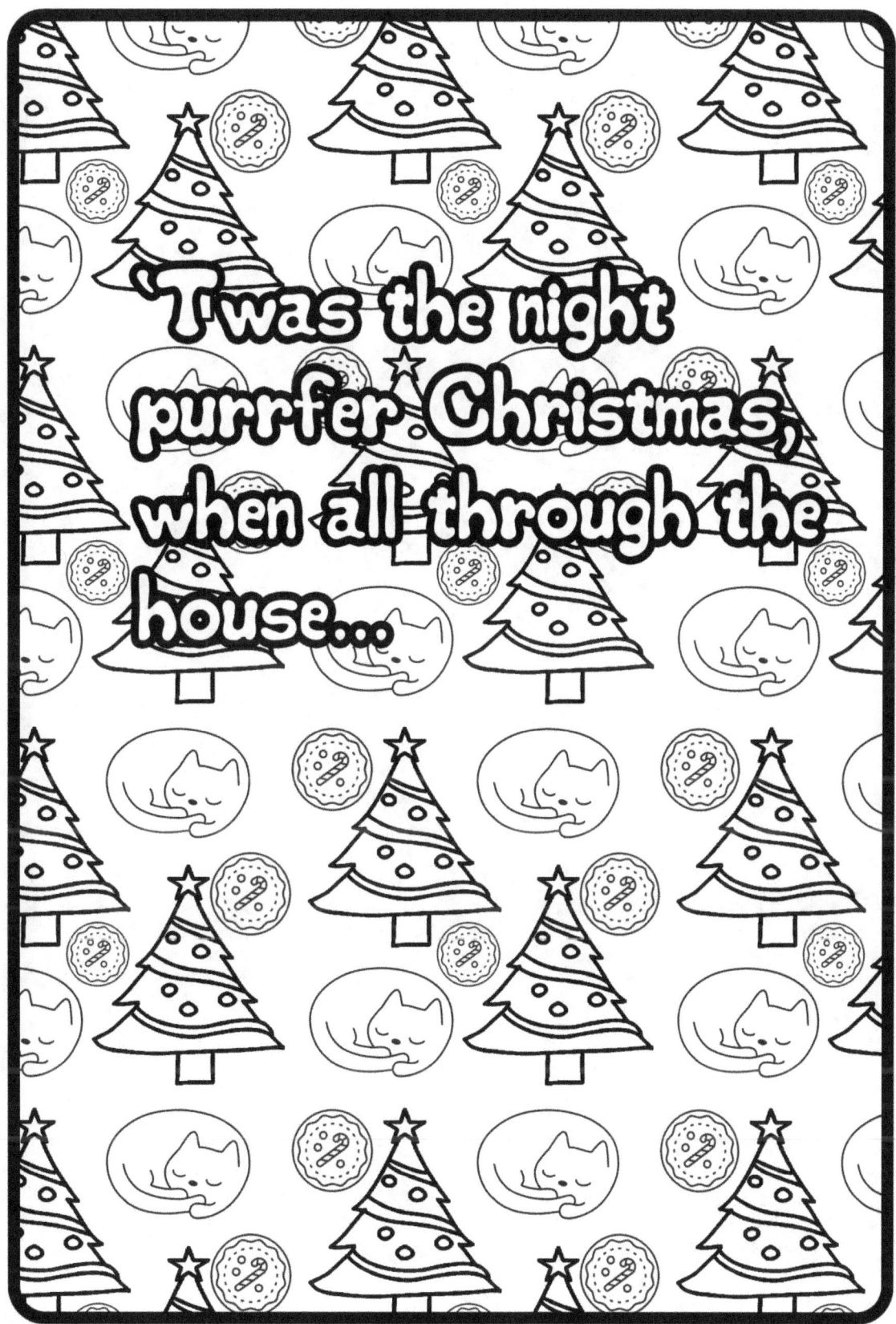

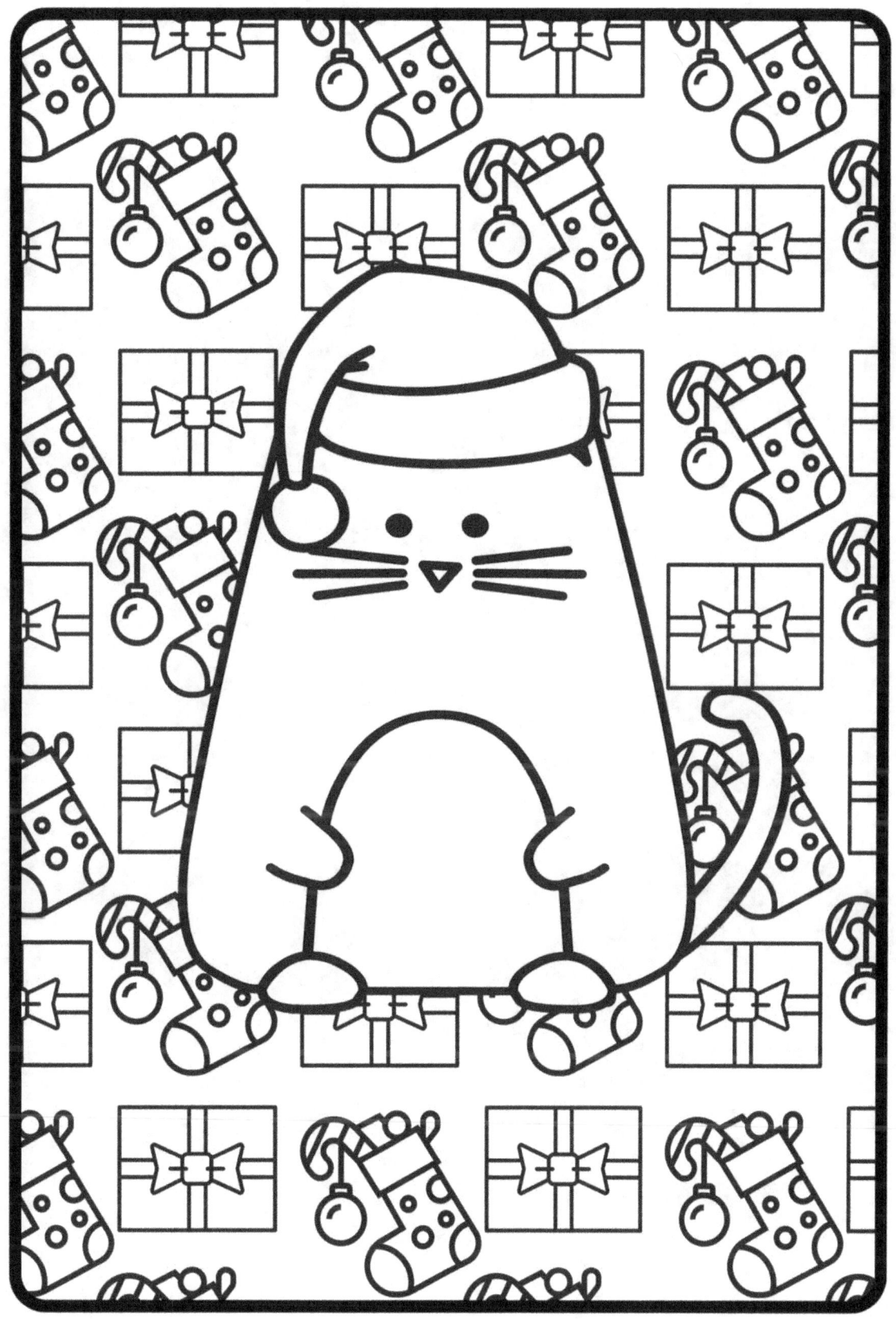

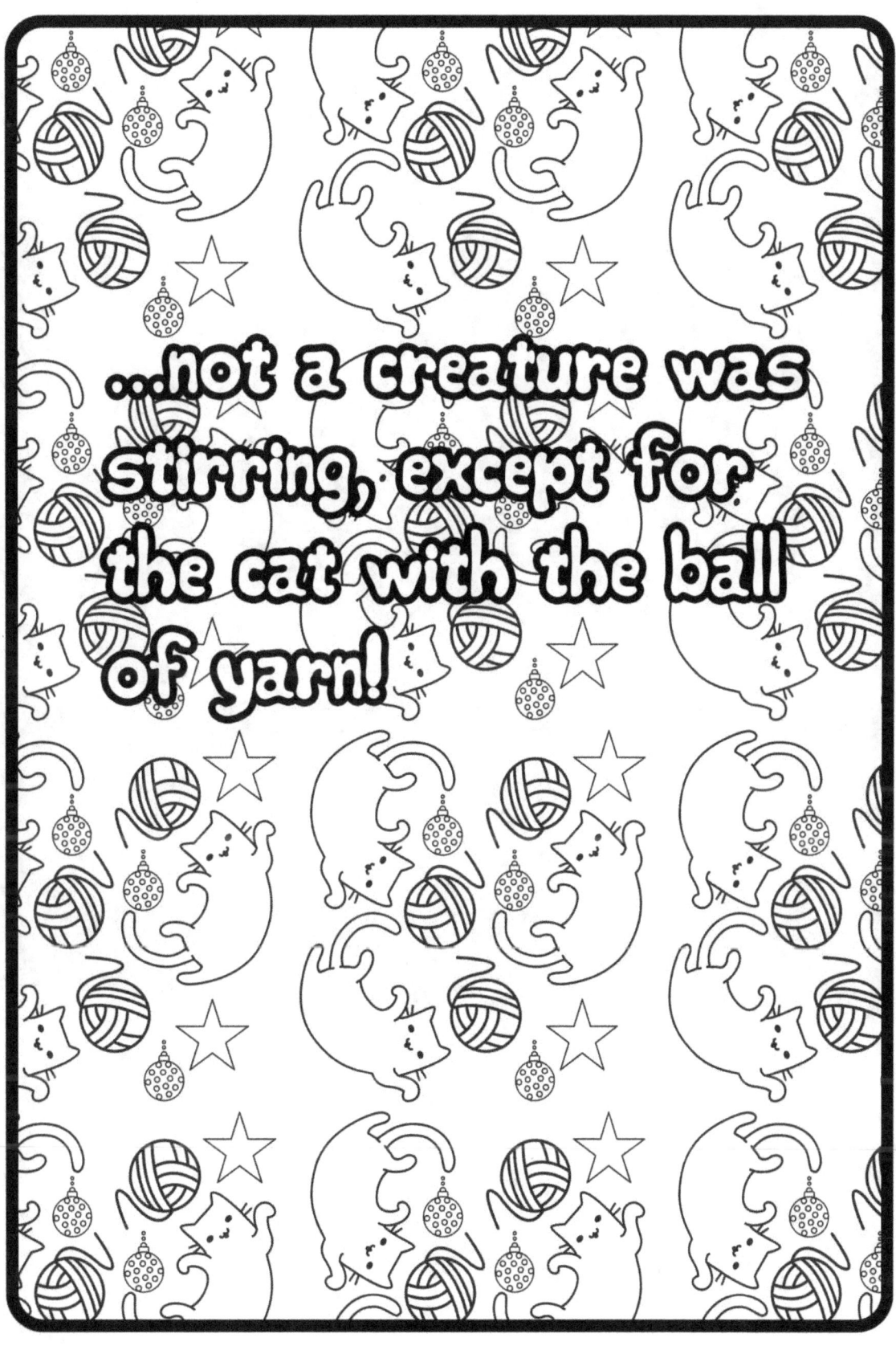

...not a creature was stirring, except for the cat with the ball of yarn!

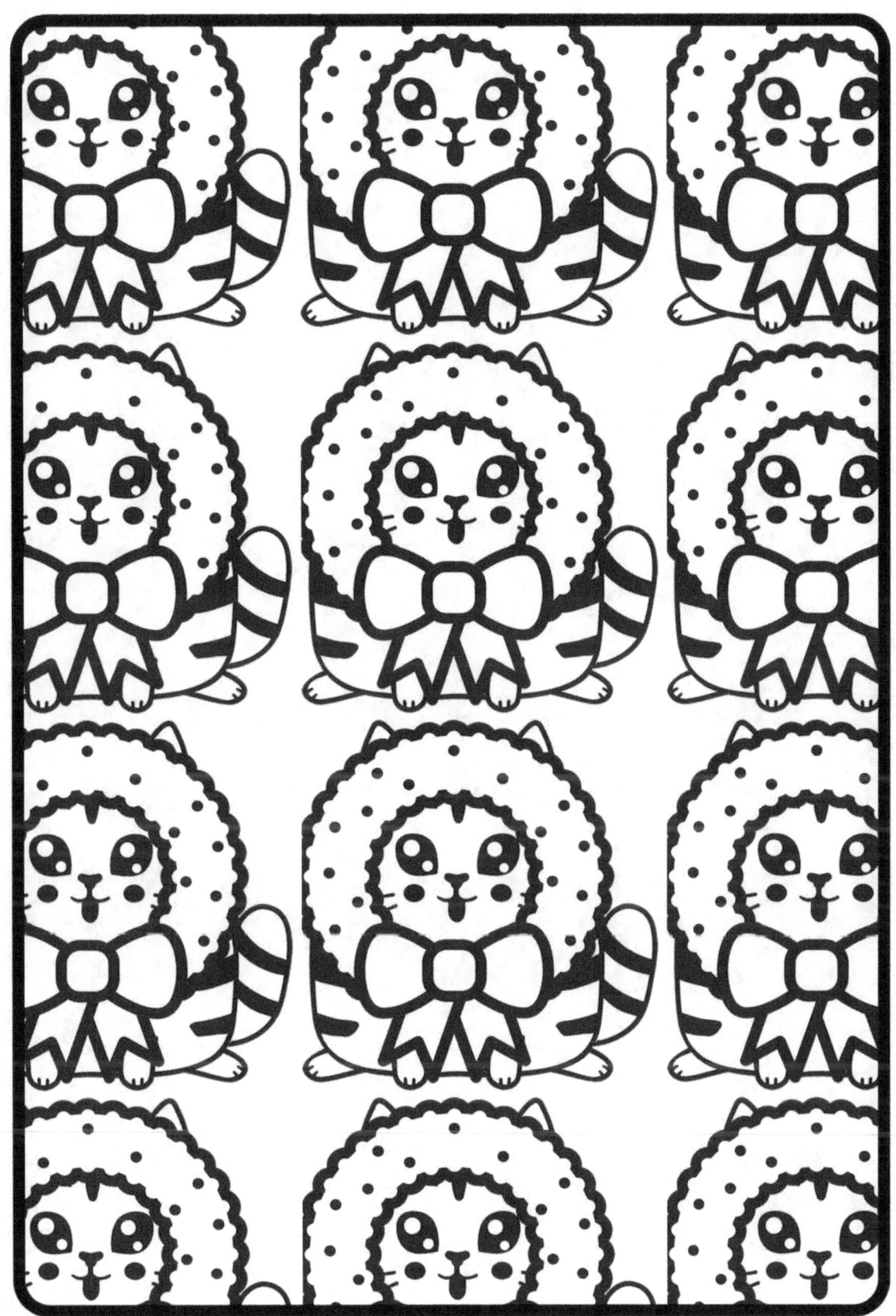

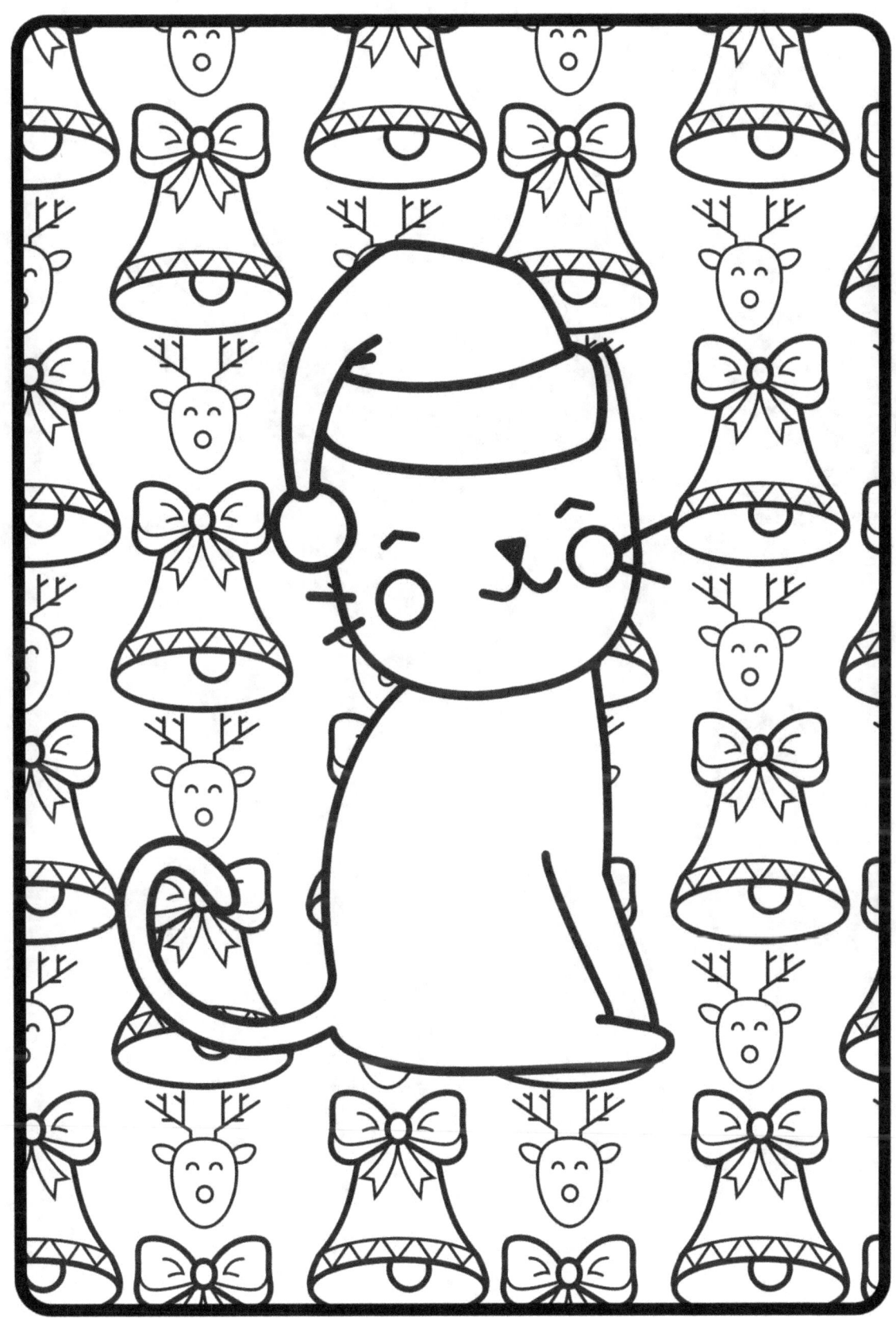

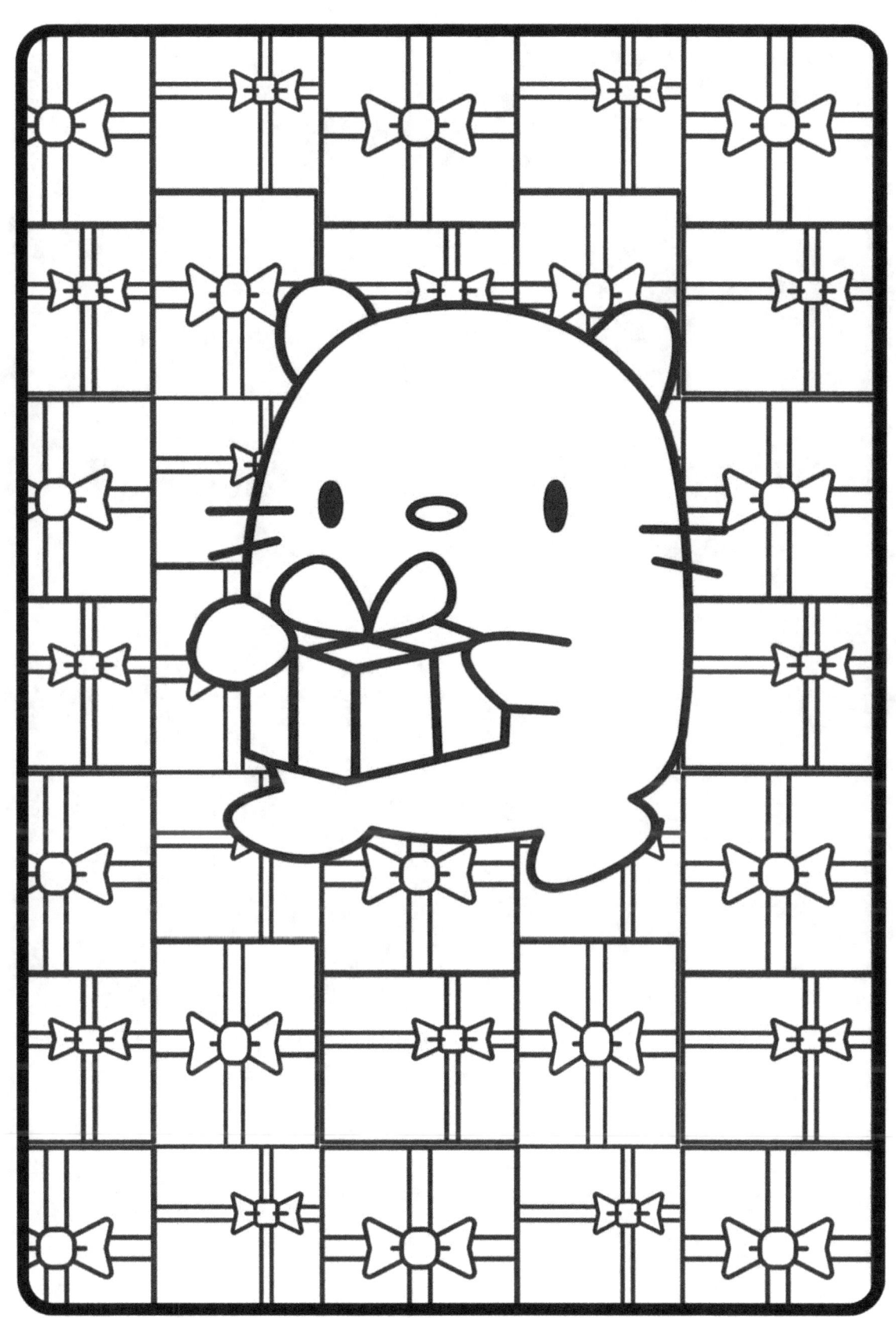

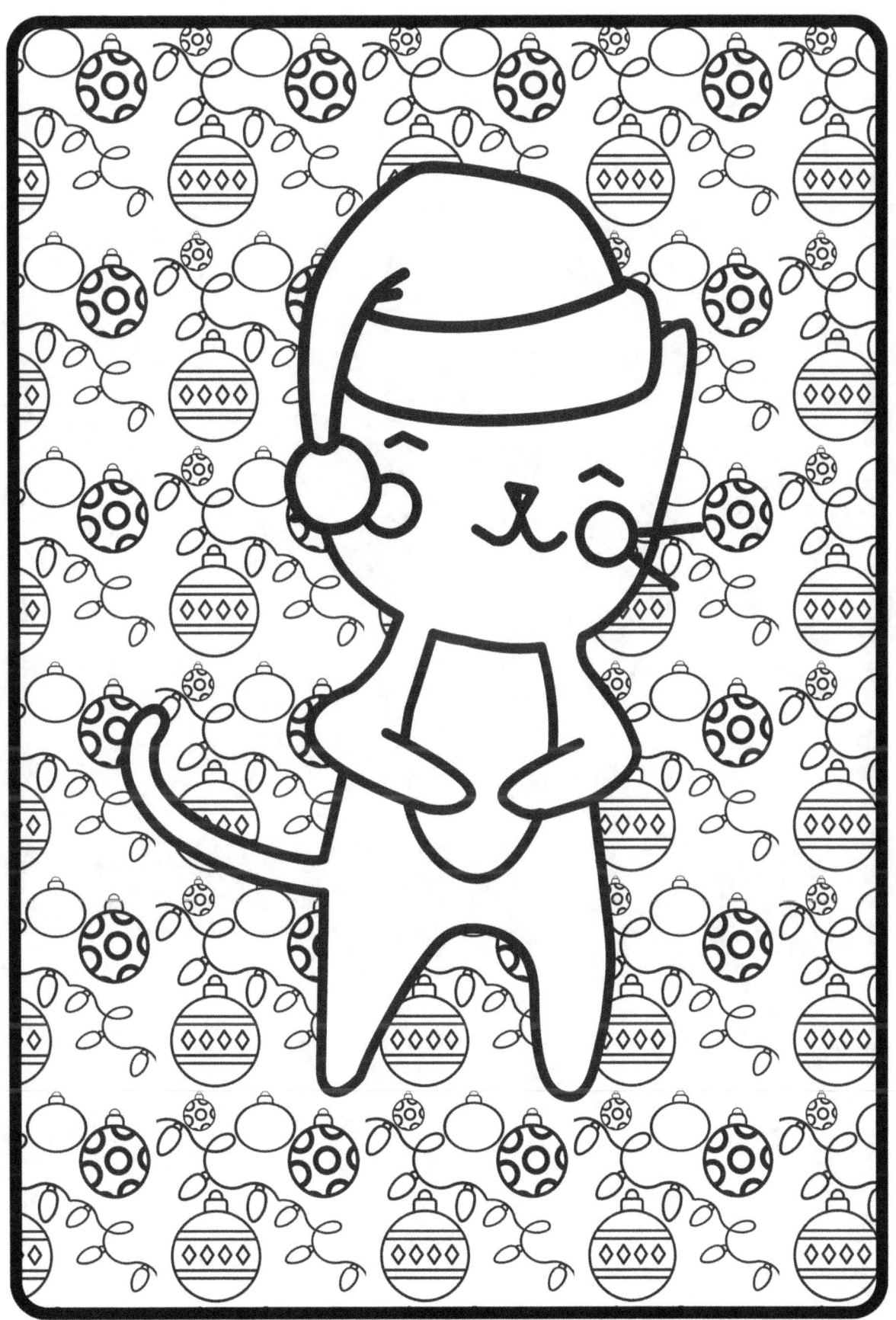

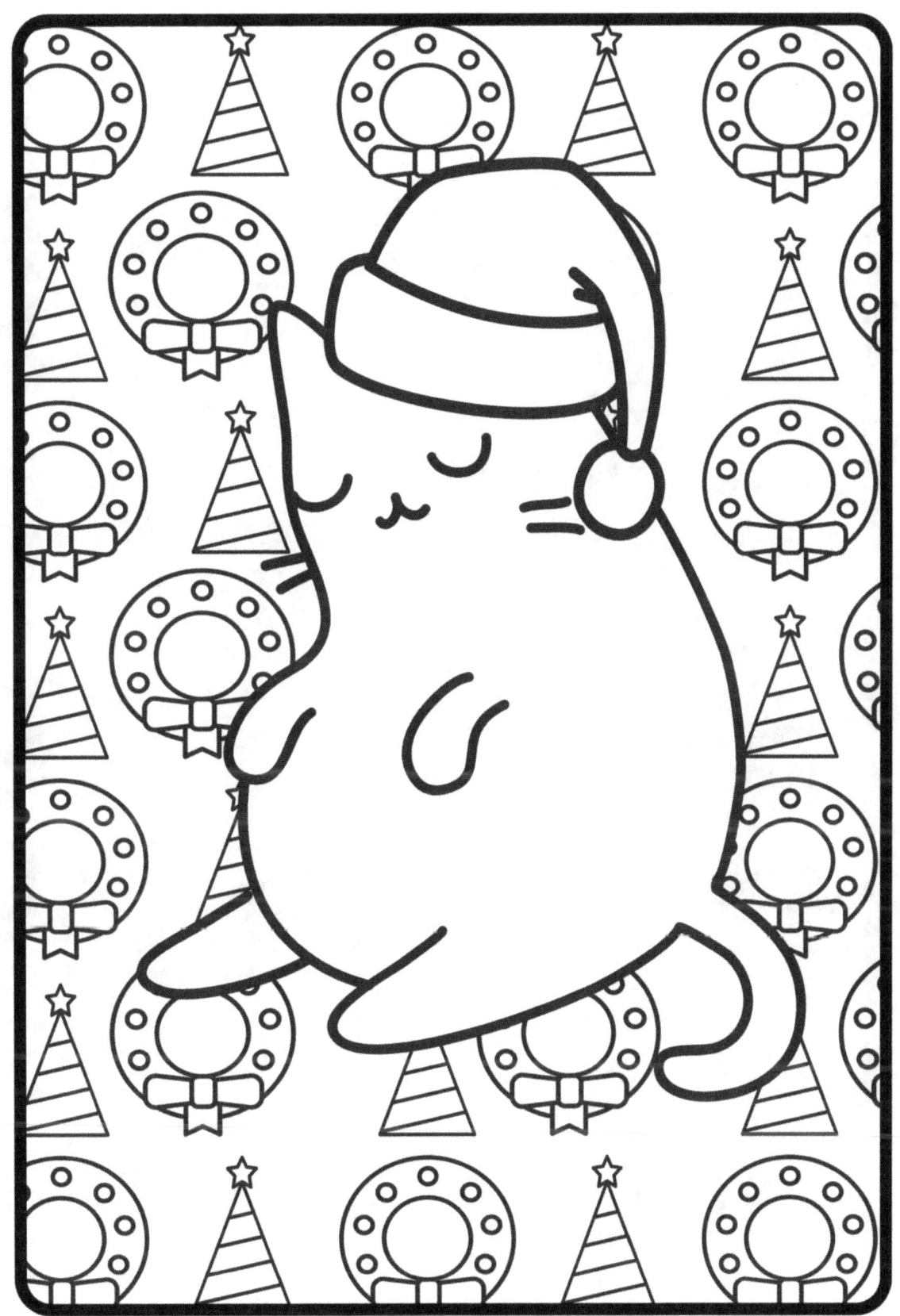

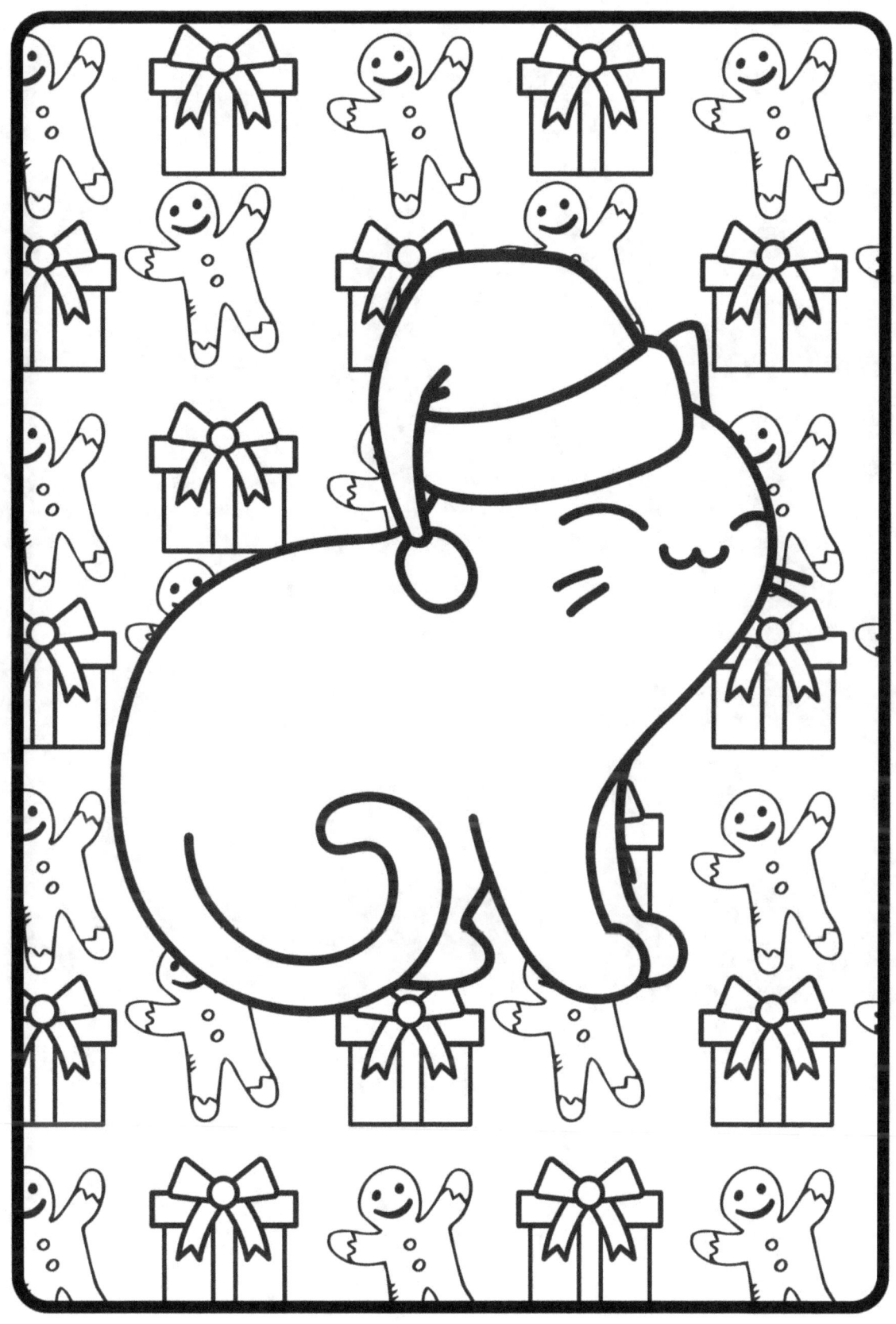

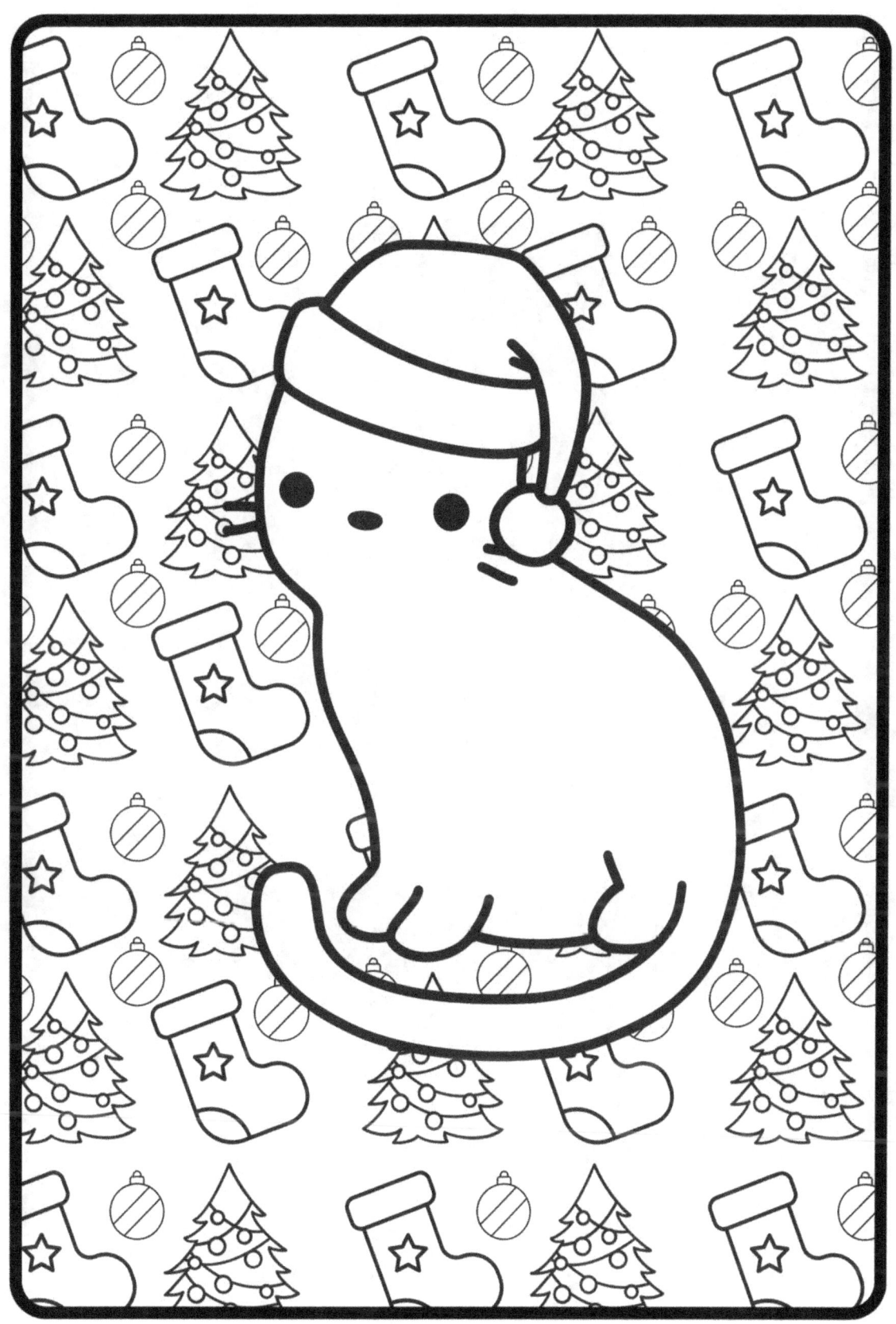

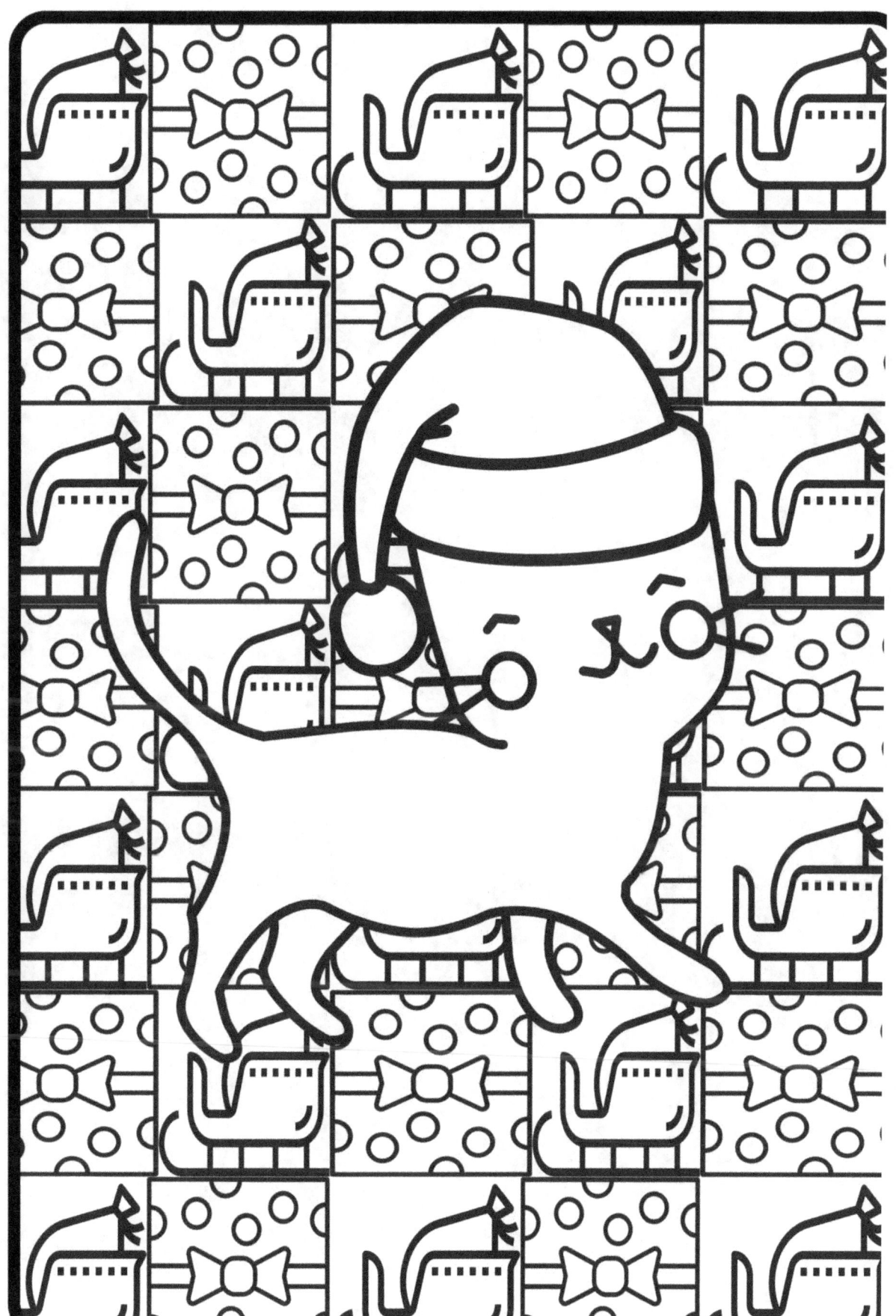

www.ingramcontent.com/pod-product-compliance
Lightning Source LLC
Chambersburg PA
CBHW080848170526
45158CB00009B/2669